Homeless on Haight

Beautiful stories of falling down, of poverty, of feeling invisible, and tales of hope on one of San Francisco's most iconic streets

Andrew Noske, PhD &
James Richardson

VERSION: 1.0.1 (updated 2023-06-01)
ISBN-13: 9798396541351

We want to dedicate this book to every person who is or was once homeless. Cold nights, cold stares, surrounded by death, a government that doesn't care and the feeling like you are invisible. You are not invisible. In a country where most people are just one accident away from homelessness, we want this book to foster love and understanding. To humanize the homeless, and to humanize the people who feel like they don't have the bandwidth to help.

And finally we dedicate this to you, for buying this book because you do care. The very modest amount of money for each copy of this book will go back into printing more books and giving just a little bit of love to the homeless.

Change will come.

-- Andrew & James

To learn more: ***www.withoutahome.net***

Preface

A whirlwind of thoughts swept my mind. After a decade as a software engineer cog in the colossal Google machine, I was laid off without warning. Cast aside via an email. For hours I let myself be sad, and wrote a ten page reflection piece entitled "*10 years of failure at Google*" that has yet to meet daylight. Yet beneath it all, I felt fortunate. Google had provided me with a good income and severance, but I had wanted to leave for years. My soul was yearning for something more meaningful. I wanted to travel to new countries, work on myself and projects deep to my core. The desensitization and disparity between the wealthy and homeless in San Francisco had been growing on my mind for years.

When afternoon came, I shook off melancholy and allowed the sunshine to coax a smile onto my face. I walked the short familiar path from my one-bedroom apartment in San Francisco to the colorful Haight street and met a homeless man called James. His smile was bright and his energy was somehow soothing and positive. His attire was worn and weathered, a flannel shirt cloaking his shoulders and a mask resting below his chin. He started talking to me, and I offered to buy him lunch. He said his teeth meant he could only really eat soft foods, so we went to a burger place and shared lunch together.

I asked him about his life. It put my own life and dreams in perspective immediately. As his story unfolded, so too did a path ahead of me. I felt moved. James told me he wanted to write books one day. I told him that we were about to write a book together. This is that book.

Table of Contents

pg24
Tony B
pg34
Sonny
pg47
Matthew
pg59
Ashel
pg64
Timbre
pg67
Murphy
pg72
Harmony
pg76
Alex
pg18
James
pg79
Father Dan

ART
FOR
SALE

Introduction

Let us set expectations from the get-go. The message of this book is one of **hope, love and breaking down barriers**, set within the backdrop of the famous, colorful and iconic Haight Street in San Francisco. It also contains several stories of **heartbreak**. It **tells the beautiful stories of seven homeless souls**, plus two formerly homeless souls, an incredible priest, and an out-of-work neuroscientist who hopes to thread these narratives together in a way that may forever change the way you look at and think about people who sleep in the cold. The **invisible people**.

James: A Dream of Authorship

In January 2023 I was living in a tent on various street corners in San Francisco. The story of how I got to the streets is explained later in the book, but the short version is I was once doing very well. Despite a very rocky childhood, I managed to move to Maui, worked hard, became a glass blower, bought three homes, found the love of my life, and got into good shape at the gym; enough to finish a 15-mile spartan race. I had an exceptional life.

On a trip to Tahoe with my friend from the gym one weekend, I was driving and things got a bit fuzzy. I asked my friend to drive and pulled off the road. I got to the back of the truck, but that's as far as I made it. I passed out and cracked my skull on the way down. I woke up in the back of an ambulance on the way to the hospital ER, where I had to spend the night.

During my overnight stay, the doctors made very little effort to determine why I fainted, but they did bill me $20k and hand me a bottle of opiates. This was the start of the spiral. My glass blowing equipment was stolen from my truck, I was taken advantage of by a once trusted family member and I got cancer. The love of my life died. She was a heroin addict. In my distraught I spent my time chasing the dragon as I gradually lost everything left, one thing at a time. Many people I know were put onto the streets after one big single unfortunate event, but for me it was **a sequence of horrible events**.

I'm sharing all of this with you so that the next time someone on the street asks you for change, you don't just see a bum, you see a person. Like you, that person has dreams and feelings. That person has people that love them. If you can help that person, that's great. If you can't afford it, that's ok. Just be sure to tell them to have a nice day. That is my only ask.

I've seen both sides of the fence. I'm a good person who has faced many challenges in this life but always comes out on top and with a smile. I won't always be on the streets. In fact, things are looking up! I've recently started delivering for Uber Eats, and I have most of the glass equipment I need to work with fire again. I've been off street drugs for over three months as of the time I wrote this, and I'm on the methadone program. This is my story.
I plan to get to a nice place, get back in touch with my daughter, and get back to my art. I also plan to write a few books before I pass away. Tomorrow is a new day. It's the first day of the rest of my life, and I'm going to do everything I can to make these dreams come true, one day at a time. Part of that plan is helping Andrew finish a book. This is that book.

Andrew: A Lucky Life

During the ebb and flow of this book, you'll read about the nature and challenge of homelessness and simple ways you might help. Before that begins, however, I will tell you about how this book came to be.

I have had a lucky life so far.

I have not been born into a life marked by crime, addiction, or poverty. My experiences in youth have been free from the traumas of rape, child trafficking, foster care, and the brutal murder of family members. I have never been subjected to persecution based on my skin color, gender or sexuality. I have never resided in an unsafe neighborhood or faced the threat of gun violence. Gang affiliations, police brutality, and physical abuse have never been part of my personal history. I have been spared the devastation of losing my entire family in a horrific car accident. Furthermore, I have not encountered any severe terminal illness or medical accidents that plunged me into financial ruin, nor have I experienced the loss of any body parts that would impede my ability to find employment.

All of these scenarios and worse have happened to people I have talked to and interviewed. This book omits many of the most brutal accounts. What remains still serves as a stark reminder that most residents of the United States are just **one big medical emergency or accident away from bankruptcy and homelessness**. We will dig into this topic more later, but just by buying this book there is a good chance you don't fall into the narrow category of thinking homeless people are lazy, or inferior to you. Any one of us could be homeless tomorrow. Even if you come from money, there are countless unlucky scenarios where you might lose your entire wealth, your physical or mental capacity and loved ones in the proverbial blink of an eye. Regardless of the hardships you might have overcome, I feel like **nobody should judge another before walking in their shoes**. Each story is as unique as the genetic codes and health that we were blessed or cursed with.

If there is one group of people in this country that are currently treated by us far worse than black people, gay people, and every other marginalized group combined... It's the homeless.

I am about to tell you a little bit about myself and repeat the word "**lucky**" an unreasonable number of times for one reason only. Even if you don't get further than the introduction of this book, I hope you shift your mindsets one step closer towards gratitude as you think about your own life.

I was lucky enough to be born in a country with great health care. Lucky enough to have parents that supported me up until university. Lucky enough that the worst thing that happened to me was my parents divorcing; which seems to happen to over half of kids these days. Lucky enough to see how lucky I am. Lucky enough to have a supportive family that encouraged me to study. Lucky enough to get a scholarship into a PhD program. Lucky to go dancing one day, and while waiting for a friend I decided to sit down and chat with a homeless gentleman for the first time. I am friendly enough that I chat to everyone, why not a homeless man? It opened my heart, I was blown away by his story, and I knew it would not be the last time.

I was lucky enough to move from Australia to the United States for a postdoc in neuroscience and then to work at Google as a software engineer. So many wonderful opportunities and projects. I was lucky enough to move to San Francisco and started "*Strawberries for Smiles*" - gifting little boxes of strawberries, socks and other items useful to homeless people[6] on my way to work on Friday. I did this not because

I'm an angel, but because I would have felt pretty lame to be in a well paid job only to become desensitized and literally step over poor people on my walk to work without occasionally being a human being. And finally, at the start of 2023 I was lucky enough to be laid off from Google. After watching the company lose its soul spark over 10 years, it wasn't a job I loved anymore and I had already been thinking about how I might make some little positive difference in this country. I wanted to try. The day after I was laid off. I walked from my one-bedroom apartment on Waller street, down Haight street, and found James. James had a warm smile and started talking to me. I was lucky to meet James, because it began the book. James is the first person I interviewed.

It's hard for me to befriend your stereotypical well paid career obsessed San Francisco resident because when they present their lives there is often a sense of entitlement. We have all met the person who not-so-subtly brags "*I went to Stanford*". How about "*I was lucky enough to go to Stanford*", to acknowledge the incredible set of events that transpired that allowed you that opportunity. When I met James he felt lucky that he was just alive. I knew we would be friends, and I told him we'd interview people and write a book about homelessness together. This is that book.

Chapter 1: The Homeless Crisis

Make no mistake, the United States has, for many years, been suffering a homeless crisis. More than half a million people experienced homelessness in America in 2022[2]. Rising housing costs, limited affordable housing options, huge economic disparities, incredibly expensive health care, mental health issues, and substance abuse all contribute to the crisis. Over 2020, the covid pandemic exacerbated the homeless problem, as job losses, evictions, and financial strains pushed more people onto the street. Despite reports that homelessness has slightly declined since the last recession, we imagine the next impending recession is likely to force another wave of people onto the street. Over 2023, new generative AI technology showed the ability to perform most computer-based jobs (coding, writing, market prediction, digital art) an order of magnitude better than humans, and thus may also cause its own new wave of unemployment. For the first time in history, it is difficult to tell our children what jobs will still be needed in the future, and how many of them may need to adapt to a life of poverty.

If this all sounds depressing, we're sorry, but things get even sadder when we specifically look at a city like San Francisco. San Francisco has more billionaires than any city, and walking down the streets is a juxtaposition of expensive cars, multi-million dollar apartments and luxury stores just one block (or less) away from people living in beat-up tents and cardboard boxes.

San Francisco has become known as ground zero for the nation's homeless crisis. This liberal and progressive city, at the forefront of societal change, paradoxically holds the highest number of anti-homelessness laws in California. For those unable to secure shelter, mere existence is criminalized.

Citizens send police to harass and arrest people living on the street, exacerbating the cycle of trauma on the streets.
This situation has transformed San Francisco into an epicenter of the national homelessness crisis, with tent cities growing, tourism declining, and human suffering escalating. This crisis affects us all, irrespective of our personal stance on it.

In 2022, the city of San Francisco estimated approximately 8,000 homeless people in the city on any given day, and about 20,000 people experiencing homelessness in the city at some point during the year[3]. For reference, that's roughly 2.5% of the city's population.

Chances are you knew around 1000 people in your high school growing up. If they all ended up in San Francisco, about 25 of them would have been homeless last year, and about 10 chronically homeless. Hearing this feels like a slap in the face with a cold fish. When we think back to high school we shudder to imagine 10 of our friends and schoolmates being homeless. Then again, few cities on earth have the ridiculously high price of living and pressure to succeed as expensive cities like San Francisco and New York. To make a dark cloud even darker, we often don't factor mortality rates into homeless statistics. People who are homeless have a 3-10 times higher chance of dying and a life expectancy of approximately 50. That's almost 30 years lower than the national average[4]. Ironically, if the US cared more to help keep more homeless people alive, the number of homeless people might be even higher. When we see someone homeless in the street we won't check if they are dead or not, and certainly won't ask them if they need help or consider the fact that this is someone's child. A human being.

At the end of day, summing up the homeless problems with statistics feels cold to me. As you get to the helping the homeless section, you'll realize there is no silver bullet solution to solve this issue. That's because everyone's story is uniquely different, beautiful and tragic. So let's take a closer look at the story of James as it represents the first interview for the book.

The Story of:

James Richardson: Writing After the Fall

Born: 1975 (48 years old) in Oakland, California.

Former life: Glass blower & owner of three properties.

About: James is a resilient and cheerful person despite the challenges thrown at him. He occasionally panhandles to make sure he doesn't ever starve, with a very friendly approach and smile. If you say no he happily wishes you a good day. Although James' clothing may hide it, he is in good physical shape for his age. He is self-conscious about his missing teeth, caused not from drugs but a rare form of mouth cancer. James is a cancer survivor with a rich history. He used to be a skilled glass blower and owned multiple homes, including a 10-acre property in Hawaii. At 38 years old, James was in the prime of his life. Then it changed.

Falling down: In 2010, James met the love of his life. Alisea. He was swept off his feet and adored her despite her addiction to certain substances. Sadly heroin would soon kill her. James lost one job and poured his money into a glass blowing shop, only to have it broken into and everything stolen. He turned to heroin, he had cancer, his own father stole from him, and gradually he liquidated what he owned to pay off debts, including a single night in the ER which cost him $20,000. Yes, America really is like that. When I met James his only possessions were stored in a green backpack, which he says is less likely to be stolen, plus he can sit on it and it keeps him fit to carry it everywhere. His most treasured possession is a journal that he keeps to talk to god and write down ideas and events from each day. James never steals but does panhandles near the WholeFoods sometimes. He feels slightly bad for panhandling, but he says you learn to lose your pride pretty quickly on the streets.

Family: After years of not talking, James is now finally close to his mother, but not his father. James has a son and daughter. He hasn't seen his daughter for 5 years, but he is happy that he can chat to her over text. By writing a book he hopes to make his daughter proud.

Aspirations: James has come off drugs, all drugs except methadone *(the drug to help you off drugs)* and weed *(the drug pretty much everyone in SF uses, even before it became legal)*. James hopes to get back onto his feet by getting a job at a glassblowing place, and often applies for work. He tells me he had a job interview yesterday, but he could tell that they judged him the second they saw his teeth. He wants an appointment to have all his remaining teeth pulled out and hopes to get dentures so people can no longer reject him based on his mouth. James wants to be seen as an equal. James is a dreamer and loves writing. He is writing two books, one on human kindness and another one as fiction. He hopes to publish and his book on kindness goes big. Finally, with a job and a little luck he hopes to see his daughter again.

CARE

Chapter 2: The Colorful History of Haight

San Francisco's Haight Street is rich in a history of vibrancy and color. The neighborhood gained fame through its diverse cultural impacts, its significant contribution to the counterculture movement of the 1960s, and its nurturing of legendary music bands.

During the Victorian era, Haight Street was a fashionable residential area, known for its ornate Victorian and Edwardian homes. These grand buildings still line the street, showcasing the architectural beauty of the time. However, it was in the 1960s that Haight Street truly became synonymous with the counterculture movement and earned its place in history. During this time the Haight-Ashbury district along Haight Street became the epicenter of the hippie counterculture. Young people from across the country flocked to the neighborhood, seeking an alternative lifestyle and a sense of community. Haight Street became known for its free-spirited atmosphere, psychedelic music, and vibrant art scene. It was a place where experimental musicians, such as the **Grateful Dead**, **Janis Joplin**, and **Jefferson Airplane** performed in iconic venues like the Avalon Ballroom and the Fillmore West.

The intersection of Haight and Ashbury Streets became the heart of the neighborhood, attracting thousands of young people who were embracing peace, love, and nonconformity. **The Summer of Love** in 1967 further solidified Haight Street's place in history, as it became a gathering place for activists, artists, and those seeking social change. The street was filled with colorful characters, street performers, and shops selling tie-dye clothing, incense, and other alternative wares.

While the intense counterculture movement eventually waned, Haight Street's colorful history continued to shape its identity. The neighborhood faced challenges in the following decades, including economic decline and social issues. However, it has also been a site of revitalization and a hub for alternative culture, art, and music scenes.

Today, Haight Street preserves its bohemian character while embracing the influences of the past. Visitors can explore a mix of vintage clothing stores, record shops, tattoo parlors, unique boutiques and cannabis dispensaries. The street retains an aura of creativity and rebellion, attracting tourists and locals alike who are drawn to its history and cultural significance. Haight Street stands as a testament to the enduring spirit of individualism, artistic expression, and social change that continues to resonate with people from all walks of life.

Few people embrace the history, quirkiness, culture and optimism of Haight street as much as Tony B Conscious. To say **Tony B Conscious** is unique and vibrant feels like an understatement. Even his name is larger than life and Tony himself, nicknamed **"The Ghetto Van-Go**", has become somewhat of an icon on Haight Street. An icon for art, for hope, for friendliness and positivity; even in the face of adversity. San Francisco itself has burned down more than once - hence the icon of a Phoenix - and similarly, Tony has moved and reinvented himself several times. Almost every day of the week, you can find Tony at the western end of Haight street, setting up his huge collection of art on the street next to an empty lot. Tony is a tall proud black man, who always dresses colorfully to the point that it's not obvious at all if he's homeless or not. But every day he spends hours packing and unpacking his art from his van onto the sidewalk, and for many hours a day he's out there in the sun complimenting and spreading positivity to everyone who walks past. Tony has this booming voice that never wavers as he wishes people a happy day, and spreads positive poetic messages. He never asks people to buy his art directly, but if they stop and look he will happily sell you any piece for whatever price you want. Many of the friendlier locals here will talk back to Tony and build a relationship over time, even if it's just a hello.

The Story of:

Tony B Conscious: The Ghetto Van Gogh

Born: 1969 (54 years old) in Seattle.

About: Tony has had several chapters in his life. His first life was in Seattle, nicknamed "Romeo" because he was a hip-hop rapper, breakdancer and ladies man. Next he moved to Hollywood and became an actor that featured in Fresh Prince and several other roles. Chapter three, he moved to Atlanta to do music and spoken word as part of the neo soul movement. Chapter four he returned to LA marking a twenty-year stint as a street artist. He also took photos of other artists around and wrote bios and published it into a book - "*Life's a Beach and Then you Die*", which you can find on Amazon. This is just one of several books he wrote. As Venice beach became denitrified, he relocated to the Bay. He hung out at Berkley and became the number one artist on Telegraph. When covid hit he came to Haigh-Ashbury to sell his artworks. Tony says he's here because he loves the history of Haight street with art and music. He says it reminds him of Venice beach, a confusing mix of beautiful history and capitalism of people trying to make money without necessarily giving back the vibration. Tony wants to give back.

When Tony talks he brims with energy. He is a constant generator of playful words, breaking into song at the drop of a hat and turns words into acronyms. He truly brings the **LOVE** ("*Living On Vibrational Energy*") (the title of one of his albums) the **ART** ("*Always Resonating Truth*"), **MUSIC** ("*Metaphysically Universal Sounds Interpreting Consciences*") and the vibes of an **MC** ("*Mostly Conscious & Major Communication*"). His street art is as colorful as he is, featuring everything from the original Black Panthers and other black icons, to Lennon, The Beatles, and various animal paintings. Tony is a master at talking to everyone. If you're interested in his art, he'll set you up with a good deal. When he's not selling paintings and making friends he's making new paintings. On a street where almost no-one makes eye contact, let alone talk to you, Tony will say hello to everyone, and there's something incredible about that. He wants to set a positive example, and is one of the few people who actually picks up litter instead of just complaining about it. Tony paints exclusively on reused materials, from recycled canvases to old skateboards and broken musical instruments, helping save the planet through conscious art and conscious action. A rare breed.

Tony's relatives sound every bit as colorful and musical as he is. His jazz legend grandparents laid the foundation of the Seattle jazz scene. His mother was a hippie, and his father, a member of the original Black Panthers. Unfamiliar with the Black Panthers, I learned from Tony about their initiative, the "*free lunch program*", and their stance against violence towards blacks, sometimes resorting to self-defense. Many were killed by police, but fortunately his Seattle-based father survived. Tony had a fascinating childhood and he credits his confidence and musical passion to his grandmother. He used to hang out at "*Pizza and Pipes*" where his grandmother played gigs in her jazz band and encouraged Tony to sing. Tony nostalgically recalls a time when

Seattle was predominantly black, home to the first Starbucks, and he casually dated a Nordstrom heiress. Once known as one of the most liberal and multicultural cities in the states, Seattle has denitrified and whitened over time.

Throughout our interview, many acquaintances of Tony said hello or joined us. We discussed San Francisco's issues and global matters, including discrimination of black people that Tony observed in Australia. Beyond his rap lyrics, Tony impresses with his profound knowledge and global perspective to those who take the time to listen.

What is the hardest lesson you learned on the streets: This is where Tony broke into rap, and I've transcribed it towards the end of the book, but to paraphrase: not everything is a blessing, but you have to stop stressing. Not everybody who says no, really means no. What you can see, you can achieve.. but you have to roll up your sleeves. Be patient. I'm out here on the corner, making it warmer.

Something you are proud of: When Tony was on Venice beach he had a son, Heru. If you ask Tony about Heru, he will grin wide and tell you Heru is his finest piece of work. A true masterpiece. He's good looking like his pop, but Tony doesn't know if he can make him hip-hop. Heru lives in Ohio, but Tony is hoping they'll be back together someday.

What tips might you offer someone newly homeless: In addition to overflowing advice Tony loves to keep a bunch of extra clothes in his car to give newly homeless people who might not have anything. Even during the interview a homeless teenager walked past who was parched, and Tony fetched him a water bottle from his van. Tony's van isn't just for storing all his art, it's full of everything he and others might need in any weather.

What are your aspirations: Tony wants to own a place, but he's the first to admit how incredibly difficult it is. Tony lives in his van and makes decent money from art, but it's never enough. If he wants to cover health care, car expenses, insurance and everything else... it would take far more than $5000 a month to cover a home. That's the cost of living in the city he wants to contribute to. To live in San Francisco comfortably, $100,000 a year is not enough.

One of the tour bus drivers happened to stop by and Tony yelled "*that's my girl Erica on the bus!*" She overheard him and shouted out "*that's my brother like there, Tony right there, the badass artist in this town, you tell them how it is!*". Tony's voice is usually booming but there was a moment after I left to grab us vegan sandwiches when he went suddenly quiet. He'd just had a deep talk with an old friend, and reflected on the fact that not everyone realizes that he is homeless. Tony takes pride in dressing up and being positive. He decides every single day to wake up positive. He says "*the second you decide the world is against you, you can die on these streets*". Tony stays clean, and works hard. He hustles harder than anyone I've ever seen. We deeply hope he makes whatever breakthrough it takes to get home one day, and see his son... but until that day and after that day, he is a beacon of hope for spreading joy. If Haight street ever loses Tony B, it will be a very sad day for the whole city. You can walk the entire length of Haight street, and the one thing you can count on is for Tony to try lifting your mood by saying hello in his big boom box voice. It isn't about making sales for Tony, he genuinely wants people to know there are some people in Haight street still trying to spread love and equality.

To get in contact and buy Tony's art:

- Tony's website: tonybconscious.com
- Tony's art: tony-bconscious.pixels.com

G

Chapter 3: Drugs, Death and Homelessness

There have been numerous books written about the history of the Haight-Ashbury, but none of them about homelessness, and few delve deeply into drugs and death.

Drug addiction, a significant contributor to homelessness, is a progressive disorder. Left untreated, it is a disorder that leads to death. To some, leaving these people untreated feels like murder. Despite this, there is a striking lack of addiction services in San Francisco. Approximately 35 detox beds for 25000 people struggling with drug addiction[6]. In 2020 alone, 712 people died from overdoses, with a shocking majority being housed individuals[6]. The city's response was to create costly "*safe sleeping areas*," yet this has failed to address the complex root issues causing homelessness. Attempts to criminalize homelessness or drug addiction do not solve the problem, they merely shift it.

The incredible "*Summer of Love*" in 1967 drew thousands of young people to Haight-Ashbury but, when the summer ended, many of these young hippies didn't or couldn't return home, and the neighborhood struggled to support them. Many became homeless. In the 1980s the nationwide economic downturn and cuts to social services under Reagan led to a big increase in homelessness across the US, including in San Francisco. Haight-Ashbury, with its reputation as a haven for alternative lifestyles, drew many of them. The 1990s and 2000s: San Francisco experienced a tech boom, which significantly increased the cost of living in the city and exacerbated homelessness, with many unable to afford housing.

Today, you'll see dozens of homeless people as you walk down Haight street, but it's honestly a really fascinating mix. Many are transient, some have mental illness, some are very much alternative lifestyle/van-life, and right in the middle, on the intersection of Haight and Ashbury, is the hangout for many of the regulars who play music, share food, share stories and be there for each other. Some of them sell art, offer to take photos for tourists, set up chairs, and sweep the area clean of litter. In a city filled with dangerous gang owned homeless tent camps, this little homeless neighborhood feels much more relaxed. A fresh change. Those that chose to hangout on Haight are often hippies and those who want to escape the darker areas of heroin overdose and gang violence in more central districts like the Tenderloin. Many of the homeless here want to spread positivity and love, despite owning virtually nothing. I would say this is what is magical about Haight-Ashbury.

The happiest people I see when I walk Haight Street are often homeless people. Depending on the time of day and week you walk Haight, the people with homes who walk this street usually look miserable and will almost never smile at you. I see a mixture of teenagers who buy expensive alternate clothes, and feel the pressure of their wealthy parents to be successful. I see career focussed hipsters making their way to the bus. All of them avoid eye contact at all costs. Life seems busy and stressful to many.

At the intersection of Haight and Ashbury, however, you can actually talk to people. This little intersection has a community, and the more I talk to people there, the more I feel recognized and welcome. A little bit of that counterculture magic is still alive.

People in Haight Ashbury may dress the part, but optimism is a complex issue. The 1960s and 1970s were marked by increased visibility and activity of biker gangs across the United

States, including notorious groups like the Hells Angels. In this period there was an unusual mix of **deadheads** (Grateful Dead fans), **biker gangs** and "**Haighters**" who would hang out in Haight street in packs and were actively rude and hostile towards tourists.

While interviewing homeless people I soon learned about just how common and saddening it is for homeless people to lose friends to health issues like cancer, violence and drug overdose each year. To learn more about drugs and death though, nobody taught me as much as Sonny. Many of his immediate family members and friends have overdosed or been murdered. He says he's lost about 22 of his friends on the street and some of those stories I have deliberately omitted.

Sonny is the epitome of a giver. In a world full of takers, there is something refreshingly warm about Sonny - who despite a lifetime surrounded by death, always offers to help others, even if it's just to offer to take your trash. He may, however, ask you to buy him a whisky sometimes. On an outside appearance, Sonny looks like he's from a biker gang, but a kind one. He used to carry around a huge knife in a sheath. I'm sure most people would be hesitant to even walk near someone with a knife and dressed like a biker, but his huge smile and friendly personality quickly lets people know that he isn't a threat to anyone, and if you learned more about his history you'd understand why he used to carry a knife.

To talk about Sonny is a huge challenge for me, because Sonny really needs his own entire book. When you sit down and really talk to Sonny you immediately realize the depth in sadness and profound messages in Sonny's story, and the stories he tells of the people he cares about. So to summarize all these stories into something short is impossible. I'm encouraging Sonny to film himself and upload some of his stories to YouTube, but let me just start with this.

Sonny was a huge inspiration for this book. The first time I saw Sonny I wasn't even living in Haight Ashbury, but I would frequent an incredible jazz cafe called "*Club Deluxe*" and Sonny was often outside, joking around with the bouncer and shooting the shit with whoever was hanging around outside. I think he enjoyed the sound of the jazz and the scene of people inside having fun though the huge glass panels. Each time I got hot from dancing I went outside to cool off and talked to Sonny if he was there. He was always quick to tell a great joke and laugh with you.

To everyone's sadness, Club Deluxe went through a long legal battle, and finally won, only to be shut down due to high maintenance costs months later. It would also be months before I moved to Haight-Ashbury and would see Sonny again. I'd ask other homeless people if they'd seen him and they hadn’t. When he finally reappeared I got to give him a hug and tell him that I'd started a book called "*Homeless on Haight*"... and since his friendliness had inspired the book, I was eager that he be one of the featured stories. Here is Sonny's story.

MOTORCYCLES
AN AMERICAN ORIGINAL

The Story of:

<u>Sonny</u>: Love, loss and biker gangs

Born: Year unknown but probably 1948s ± 2 years (~75 years old) in Olongapo in the Philippines.

About: Sonny's history is colorful and rough. Sonny was born in Olongapo in the Philippines, which at that point was a known hotbed of crime, unrest and sex for sale. Olongapo is the place where all the surrounding US naval base people go to "*party*". It was a rough town where people were told to hide their necklaces else it would be stolen, and it wasn't unheard of for people to shoot children and common for adults to ask to have sex with children. Sonny reflects that his life was always felt surrounded by "*a lot of death*" and that started early. He's the most cruel thing done to human beings, and seen the abusers walk away smiling. Sonny doesn't know who his real parents are, but suffice it to say that Olongapo has its own word, "*Amerasians*", for a group that bears the stigma of orphanage and prostitution. It was a cruel childhood.

One fateful day a group of American men came to Olongapo and discovered a very young white boy with incredible blue eyes, who couldn't speak a lick of English. Fortunately the men and the boy all spoke some Tagal (Filipino). The boy had no idea who his parents were and it was clear he was being sold off. Someone associated with the Hudson family (as in the "*Hudson Bay Trading Company*") bought him up for adoption to get him off the street and suddenly Sonny was growing up in the area with three different dads to help raise him right in this rough murderous neighborhood. One of these three adopted dads was ***Sonny Barger***, the famous American outlaw biker and a founding member of the Oakland, California chapter of the Hells Angels Motorcycle Club. It was through his respect for his adopted son that Sonny ended up with his first name "*Sonny*".

Sonny wouldn't come to the US till after the Vietnam war was over. An Air Force intelligence officer helped adopt him into the country but it was an immediate issue that he didn't have a proper birth certificate. At various points Sonny recalls that people wanted to cut off his benefits and one investigator who asked him "*who are you really, nothing matches up for you?*". Maybe it adds to the sense of mystery, but a little research on Olongapo's history might give you the hard truth about what can and has happened near several US naval bases overseas. Sonny had found the means to move to the United States and in 1976 (late 20s) first came to San Francisco. Sonny eventually found work, found love, got married and moved out of San Francisco to work in security all over the country. New York, Florida, Atlanta and Chicago were just a few cities he lived and worked in. Sonny would soon be working as head of security for big bars and restaurants. Thanks to his people skills, he was often employed for limited time to venues when there was a killer or rapist in town. Sonny would be amazing to talk to everyone inside the venue and prostitutes in the area to help identify or at least keep away the source of danger. One of his toughest jobs was head of security for a set of three bars during a world fair in New Orleans in 1984. Sonny built a reputation and someone that could be counted on to keep patrons safe and happy. His proudest gig was when he was given "*The Firehouse*" New Orleans to manage. He was living in the apartment upstairs, and there was an actual fire pole he could slide down into the bar to get to work in the morning.

The happiness didn't last. After a big climb, Sonny was about to receive a huge blow. Sonny's wife was raped while he was at work. When he returned she wasn't there and then he was told to please call the pastor, who had somehow discovered what had happened. During this assault, his wife contracted aids, and her parents came to help. She died six months later. Sonny was devastated.

After Sonny's wife passed, Sonny returned to San Francisco. So deep was his depression that friends helped keep him distracted and drunk so that he wouldn't commit suicide. But Sonny couldn't handle the pain. Sonny hatched a plan to escape to Blue Lake with a shotgun to end his own life in privacy. To go quietly into the night. He would disappear deep into the woods and all they would ever find of him would be bones. Fate had other ideas.

Sonny was sitting on the edge of a river on the day of his planned suicide and looking at happy families on the other side. The life he didn't have. The water levels were particularly high after rain, and a family passed by on a white water kayak tour. Suddenly a woman hit an eddy, capsized and she got trapped underwater by a tree. Onlookers screamed, helpless to intervene from the side of the river. Not fearing death, Sonny threw aside his walking cane, dived in, fought the current and managed to get to her. He held her out of the water and eventually they threw him a rope. Sonny kept the woman on top of him and got her to safety. As they neared the shore, Sonny's grasp slipped. Swept downstream, he struck his head, lost consciousness and suffered spinal injury. Sonny would regain consciousness and spend the next six months in a hospital.

Sonny never did get to hear a thank you from the family, but in the hospital he realized that he had reason for living. To help people in need. Sonny very modestly told me: "*I planned to commit suicide that day. I realized that I didn't save that woman's life. She saved mine*". He said he was sad he'd never get to thank that woman for saving his life. Fate intervened. Sonny's words and emotion made me cry during the interview and just writing these words down is causing me to cry again.

Sonny pulled himself out of depression. It was at this time Sonny started hoping with the "*Compassionate Release Program for Dying Inmates*". It was rough work, and obviously surrounded by death, but his hope was that there was sometimes a chance to have prisoners released to hospice to enjoy slightly better dignity in their last years or moments of life. Within a single year period, Sonny was able to get 15 inmates out of prison and it was clearly one of the most incredible things he, or anyone, could have done with their life. Just to let someone know that, despite their life mistakes, they could enjoy some dignity and self reflection in the last moment of their life. Sonny had effectively already decided that the remainder of his life would be devoted to helping others, and instead of going deeper into all the details of Sonny's life and other tragedies, this is a good point for us to fast-forward to the present day.

Sonny teared up often when relaying certain parts of his life, as did I. And so the interview was spaced over three sessions. At points he talked so fast, I needed to (for the first time) bring out my laptop and try to type quickly to keep up. I am almost certain I have small pieces of the story wrong, and there are honestly moments of his story that seem surreal... like they were imagined. How could Sonny possibly have met so many famous people for instance? Well working security in New York can do that! I'm not here to tell all of Sonny's side stories about famous musicians and their children though. I would often have to prompt Sonny to return to his own story. But then again. Sonny's story is absolutely intertwined with the people he cares about.

Twice while chatting with Sonny on the street, and once while sharing a beer, the famous local Father Dan walked past and Sonny waved him to come over so we all do fist bumps and cracked a couple of jokes. Sonny loves singing the praises of Father Dan and raves about "*the positive transformation that Father Dan, and his attitude, and the way he engages his kids on the street... has been overwhelming*". Sonny has an impressive vocabulary. I've heard him use amazing words like "*demonstrous*", but I think "*overwhelming*" is one of Sonny's favorite words. He uses it with emphasis. Overwhelming. He tears up a little every-time he talks about someone that has done great good in the world, or someone that has done great bad. Sonny is quite versed with Father Dan's story and says that the father's only sin is doing crosswords in a pen. And for that he joked to Father Dan he should beg the lord for forgiveness every night.

More than anything, Sonny loves to talk about "*his kids*". It feels like Sonny knows everyone. Over the last few years he's seen 22 of his kids die in the Haight area alone, many more if he counts and LA and other areas he visits. Many of them overdosed, some hit old age and medical issues, some were murdered, some were raped and murdered. All these stories should be written down in my humble opinion. Lives lost that have all deeply affected Sonny, and you can see it when his eyes water up. Despite all the laughs we have, this interview was tough. I've never really interviewed people in my life, so I don't know the rules, but I like to think I've done an okay job of letting Sonny pause.

Sonny's "*kids*" know him well, and help take care of him. Sonny has a small income from a pension, and knows people who can help him get a bus ticket if he wants to catch the Greyhound bus or Amtrak between Los Angeles and San Francisco. He has a system. Sonny is definitely nomadic, at times he's owned a car, but often they get towed. I mean this is San Francisco. Sonny says he usually sleeps wherever, sometimes people will take him into a motorhome, sometimes in the woods. He seems happy to say that he usually has a pillow under his head. One of the kids nicknamed him "*Growling bear*", he doesn't like to be poked in the morning! At the end of one of our interviews, I gave Sonny some money as I knew he would immediately take that money and buy some food for all the kids hanging out on the corner. I find the words "*kids*" amusing, because they are not all youngsters, but I guess compared to Sonny, they might seem like youngsters. The average life expectancy of someone homeless in San Francisco is only 50 and so Sonny is well above that.

Sonny has talked to so many people about their stories. He often feels like he can't share the stories of pain that he's had. I'm glad that he did though. I only wrote a fraction of these stories down. Sometimes it was important to just listen. When I first saw Sonny again after a long period away, he had been in hospital in LA. He had gotten very sick and realized he didn't know how many years he had left. He cried a little when I walked up to him and said I had started interviewing some of his fellow homeless folk - his kids - to write a book. He told me when he thinks of death he still wants to make a positive difference in the world. I told him he already has. To me, between the woman's life he saved, the dozens of people he pulled out of jail to regain dignity, the countless people he's helping in many ways... Well there are few people in this world who have touched as many hearts already as Sonny.

Sonny people stories: I'm just picking just one "*Sonny story*" about another person, to drill home that there is a great prejudice on the streets. The story is a black boy called Kong. Kong used to hang out near Flipping Burger, and when the crew first found him he was dressed in a terrible way, sweatpants and stained, so Sonny and the boys got together to help buy some clothes and dressed him. At the time, Kong was sleeping outside people's houses on the street - not in a tent - and peed into a 5 gallon bucket. Sonny watched as one resident took that bucket while

Kong was asleep, and poured it all over him. Sonny tells me there is a passage in the bible about God knowing "*every grain of sand*". When Sonny and the boy's first saw Kong he looked like a road kill, but they saw potential and dressed him up. And yet, to someone else, they saw human garbage. Sonny tells me he can deal with people who see the homeless as visible, but it hurts his heart to see people treat someone like trash. Sonny himself has also had people who live in the neighborhood deliberately urinate all over his stuff to show that he was not welcome. And he says, plenty of people in shops tell him outright that he is garbage, just because he is in homeless attire. In the same streets where you have an amazing man like Father Dan, you have these awful people. It hurts his heart. People can be treated worse than invisible, in a supposedly progressive place like San Francisco.

What is the hardest lesson you learned on the streets: Sonny says his hardest lessons were actually indoors. When things go wrong in relationships, you are stuck there, you can have people with monstrous behavior and you can't just leave. His hardest lessons were from people who on the outside looked like they wanted to be loving and nurture and care for him. But often these people did the opposite.

Something you are proud of: Sonny says he's proud of his unofficial father Ralph (Sonny Berger). Barger was instrumental in unifying various disparate Hells Angels chapters and had the club incorporated in 1966. Barger served a total of 13 years in prison, following a conviction for cocaine trafficking, but Sonny says he was a decent man who got throat cancer, and in the last years of his life was able to atone for any sins and ride out of life with a clear conscience.

What tips might you offer someone newly homeless: To keep doing good for others, and stay peaceful always. "*Violence is the last resort of a desperate individual who's stopped using commonsense*".

What are your aspirations: To write books. "*I know I have at least 5-6 books in me*". If it makes money, some of it would go to buy some of the kids some prefab houses, and some would go into Slab City, an unincorporated, off-the-grid alternative lifestyle community in the Sonoran Desert in California. Aside from that "*just continue what I'm doing, there isn't a reason to change*".

Sonny's reading recommendations: I haven't done "watching recommendation" for anyone else, but I really love the Sonny told me a list of three books I should read: (1) "*Black like me*", a story about prejudice in the 60s, (2) "*Jonathan Livingston Seagull*", a story about freedom and self-realization, and the "*The Art of War*" by Sun Tzu. He says the one movie everyone should watch is "*Pay it Forward*", which he hopes would have a ripple effect on the world.

While Sonny has lost many of his kids to drugs, he knows that Haight-Ashbury is one of the safer areas for homeless people to gain some distance from the hard drugs and gangs in the center of SF that surround the homeless housing areas. While many people may die of health conditions, meth and heroin remains one the greatest threats to young people on the street. The despair of feeling alone and abandoned can easily turn from one drug to another. This is a story well known by James, and captured in his poem about Alisea.

Poem: Nasty ol dragon

Rock your baby
to and fro,
All the lost children,
Nowhere to go
Chasing the dragon,
Playing the part
Seeking love from the needle,
Till it poisons your heart
Last i saw you,
With tears we did part
That nasty ol dragon,
Tore us apart

In my dreams,
Still together we are,
for ever and ever
Dreaming always of the great bright yellow,
As i lay my head down on my concrete pillow
Loving her all ways,
Never forget
That pretty little flower,
That very last kiss
Hold you so close,
So near to my heart
We will meet again,
In the great white abyss
Now let's dim the lights and embrace with a kiss
So the time may pass faster,
I'm sorry to say
It may be a long time,
Before we can play
I've now got a purpose, and now a good reason to stay here for some time though I know you will wait,
For whatever season in whatever year,
No matter the time, I will see you again, no reason no rhyme
With Jezebel's power,

With Beelzebub's vanity,
Made way for the dragon,
To slayeth your sanity
In purgatory for now,
For what seems like forever
You will wait by the gate for the horse to ride by, the white horse will gallup,
And I am the rider
Swooping you up on the mount,
The mount by my side
Off into the sunset,
Alas together we'll ride as I swallow my pride one last time,
Always my heart,
My love unconditional,
Not jealous, so kind never will die nor the not will unbind,
Patience my virtue,
I never left her behind
She will stay in my heart,
Till ends be of time...

-- James Richardson

AK033
things Alone
call me

Chapter 4: The Real Crime

The rate of crime varies widely from one neighborhood to the next in San Francisco. Wealthy suburbs like the Marina, Presidio Heights, Pacific Heights, Noe Valley, the Inner Sunset, and the Outer Sunset have the lowest crime rates and strong police presence. The most dangerous suburb in San Francisco is the notorious Tenderloin District, followed by areas like the Mission District, Outer Mission, Hunters Point, Western Addition and South of Market (SOMA).

The city has been particularly associated with a high rate of property crimes, especially car break-ins or "smash and grab" thefts. All housed residents in San Francisco know well that leaving anything visible in your car is a sure fire way to have your window smashed. Even if you leave your window down, some of my friends who live in San Francisco have had more smashed windows than they can count. If you explore San Francisco, it's a good idea to know which streets are the most dangerous at night. Drug, gang violence, rape and murder does happen, but seems to happen mostly to the poor. The police-force is spread thin in many neighborhoods and if someone homeless is raped or murdered, it gets an entirely different reaction from police than if someone from wealth is raped or murdered. This isn't even debatable. It just is.

Several homeless people in the mission, in their desire to feed themselves and family will steal food and other items from local shops. These stolen items are just sold openly in streets in the mission. The real crime, as far as I'm concerned however, is that the city is unable to clean up the drug problem in the Tenderloin. In the places with the most homeless shelters, there are the most overdoses. Counter-intuitively sheltered is often a death sentence, precisely because there is violence and drug dealers just outside your complex. Statistics on this phenomenon are hard to come by, but when you interview homeless people, this seems to be a popular consensus. Living in a tent or cardboard box around Haight Street gives you a longer life expectancy than some of the sheltered houses.

A sad stigma against the homeless, of course, is that they turn to theft to survive. Sometimes the obsession of an addict to get their new fix might make them try to score money from dark alleys in central San Francisco, hence residents should be street smart. I have never really felt unsafe in Haight-Ashbury however. I really do think the true crime here is the mismanagement of the homeless population.

Most homeless people I have talked to in my neighborhood seem like overwhelmingly good people who do the right thing. One classic example of a standup citizen is Matthew.

I met Matthew Hay-Chapman in 2015. I was exploring Golden Gate Park in San Francisco with two friends visiting from the Ukraine. Matthew was sleeping on a bench in the park not far from Haight-Ashbury. I only had $5 left in my wallet, but I approached Matt, put the money in his shoe, shook his hand and we chatted a little. I said that I wished to hear his life story, but I could also see that he was tired from a long day, and I had to get back to my friends so I gave my email address, and within the next couple of days he emailed me his story. This is Matthew's story.

The Story of:

Matthew Hay-Chapman: *Homeless Hero*

Born: 1961 (~62 years old) near Reno.

About: Matthew, hails from the mountainous region near Reno, Nevada, and was raised in a large Catholic family with ten siblings. The son of a career U.S. Air Force serviceman, Matthew's roots trace back to the San Francisco-Berkeley area where his parents originated. When I first interviewed Matthew he was 55 and was reflecting on his past life as a Carpenter and Building Engineer.

Matthew's pride shines through when speaking about his son, Allan, and daughter, Sarah. Sarah, despite being born premature with severe cerebral palsy, hydrocephalus, and intellectual disability, radiates resilience. Sarah, now a woman, resides in a state home for the disabled due to a severe gag reflex that prevents her from consuming food or drink. Allen is a gifted artist who sadly lost custody of his children to the Oregon Child Welfare Protective Services but Matthew lives to visit his grandchildren whenever he can afford it.

Matthew himself has faced adversity over the past 18 months. Health issues forced him to leave his position as a night manager at a boutique hotel in Union Square, and he found himself without a home in the bustling streets of San Francisco. During this challenging period, he made several trips to Oregon in a failed attempt to secure temporary custody of his grandchildren, who sadly entered the foster care system.

Presently, Matthew is wrestling with severe anxiety, depression, and peripheral neuropathy affecting both his feet. These issues trace back to a lower-back injury he sustained in a work-related incident 15 years ago, which resulted in a bulging disc and stenosis. Fear of a potential diabetes diagnosis looms over him, adding to his health concerns.

Despite a deep-seated phobia of doctors and an innate reluctance to prioritize his health, Matthew has recently sought medical assistance to manage his severe pain. His journey is overwhelming and filled with trials, but Matthew remains resilient, drawing breath and navigating the labyrinth of life's crises. His story is a testament to human endurance, with hope shining like a beacon, inviting help and understanding from those willing to reach out.

Hard-luck hero: In 2016, not long after the first interview, Matthew sent me an article by the San Francisco chronicle reading "*Hard-luck hero helped police nab dangerous escapees*". It was a wonderful story! In summary:

Matthew Hay-Chapman, a 55-year-old homeless man residing in Golden Gate Park's botanical garden, played a pivotal role in helping the San Francisco police capture two escapees from an Orange County jail due to his avid interest in current events. Despite dealing with personal tragedies and severe back pain, Matthew stayed informed by frequently visiting the library and reading newspapers at a local McDonald's. His keen eye and news knowledge led to the recognition of the fugitives, earning him a $140,000 reward. Despite hardships, Matthew's attention to detail and commitment to doing what's right led to his heroic actions. Recognizing a suspicious van from news reports, he carefully observed and followed one of the fugitives, Hossein Nayeri, before alerting nearby police. His vigilance resulted in the successful apprehension of Nayeri and a second fugitive, Jonathan Tieu. Nayeri, who had been held on aggravated mayhem, kidnapping and torture charges, and Tieu, who was facing gang-related murder and attempted-murder charges, were returned to authorities in Orange County. Matthew now hopes to use the reward money to improve his own circumstances and help his troubled family. His actions stand testament to his sharpness, resilience, and innate goodness, even in the face of personal adversity.

Ongoing Trouble: The photo earlier is Matthew posing for the article, still proudly wearing the black hoodie that San Francisco police gave him as thanks for his assistance. That is where the article ended, but in subsequent emails Matthew sent me, he talked about how difficult it was to get the money he was promised, and his ongoing health conditions. In the United States, even a hundred of thousands dollars won't cover you for serious medical conditions. Matthew has been hard to get hold of, but my hope is to interview him again before this book is published. Matthew is the first homeless person who's story of homelessness I asked for and published on my little blog on the internet. I hope I get to hand him a copy of this book soon. I can't imagine all the adversity he's been through, and he stands as an example of how health issues can quickly put a hard working person on the street, and of how someone down on their luck can still fight hard to keep the word safer for others. It's also a huge story about how someone's luck can shit positively or negatively in a moment. My last correspondence with Matthew was that he was still homeless and sometimes hangs out in Haight-Ashbury, so hopefully we will meet soon.

Chapter 5: Helping the Homeless

"Give a man a fish, and you feed him for a day. Teach a man to fish, and you feed him for a lifetime."
-- famous proverb.

When I first searched "*how to help the homeless*" on Amazon in 2018 I was surprised how little literature I found. One of the only guidebooks I found was "**Helping the Homeless: A Service Guide**" by Chaplain T. M. Babcock[1]. It is a wonderful insightful book for anyone wanting to help, and it mentioned socks as one of the most valuable things you can give someone who is homeless. People on the streets are on their feet constantly. That's why I started my little www.strawberriesforsmiles.com project - gift little boxes with strawberries (full of vitamin C), socks and other little useful knick-knacks on my walk to work.

If you want to help the homeless, we're not necessarily suggesting you give boxes full of strawberries or socks though. A helpful part of any homeless project is making sure homeless people feel seen. Any gesture of kindness gives a glimmer of hope their country hasn't completely turned its back on them. Even if a wealthy government like the U.S. government feels like it has abandoned them, the kindness of people like you might be their best shot and pulling themselves up. Here's five great tips:

1. Volunteer to local organizations
This can be a homeless shelter, soup kitchen, or non-profit organizations that help the homeless. These groups have the experience, resources, and systems in place to provide direct aid. Your time, funds, or donated items can go a long way in helping them achieve their goals.

2. Be kind and smile
People experiencing homelessness are stigmatized, and in many cases, criminalized. Not having the means to get a proper meal, shower or do laundry can result in a lot of shame, and by ignoring people experiencing homelessness on the streets, we only further their sense of disconnection from society at large.

Because of how difficult it can be to acknowledge an individual who is suffering, many of us tend to ignore someone when they ask for help. While you never have to give cash if that's not something you're comfortable with, simply acknowledging people experiencing homelessness with eye contact or a smile can go a long way. Be polite and try to engage as you can, and always be mindful of your personal safety and avoid taking unnecessary risks if someone appears mentally unwell.

3. Educate yourself and others
According to the latest San Francisco Homelessness Point-in-Time Count and Survey, the top causes of homelessness are job loss, addiction, family conflict, eviction, divorce and illness – factors that are outside of an individual's control. Generally, homelessness is not a choice. By educating yourself and others about circumstances that lead to homelessness, you will help stop the misconception that people choose to live on the streets.

The "Beyond Homeless"[7] project (beyond homeless.org) has an incredible short video called "Beyond Homeless: Finding Hope" which explains the state of homelessness and wealth disparity in San Francisco, and a solid plan to actually solve the issue. If you have any influence in policy you should watch the film now!

4. Hand out toiletries, snacks or resource guides

Many people experiencing homelessness don't have access to necessities like toiletries or healthy food. Carrying and handing them out is a tangible way you can help. Consider getting together with a group of friends during the day and offering kits that contain things we all need daily, such as packs of tissues, hand sanitizer, a toothbrush and toothpaste, deodorant, band aids, snacks or even a reusable water bottle. You can also carry information on local homelessness services and offer those to people who ask for or appear to need help.

5. Donate to an organization doing work to end homelessness

There are many amazing organizations across the Bay Area working to effectively and efficiently address homelessness. Why do we still see so many people on the street then? San Francisco's housing crisis has exacerbated homelessness in recent years, and even the best of these organizations typically does not receive enough funding to meet the level of need in the city.

Poem: One Accident Away

One accident away, a thread so thin,
The land of opportunity, in a game that few win.
Most live paycheck to paycheck, nervous the whole way,
Student loans or credit card debt, haunting each day.

The teacher, the waiter, the nurse on the floor,
All dancing a rhythm, near the poverty door.
Every month a tightrope, every day a gamble,
In life's cruel circus, where hopes often scramble.

In the constant hum, and a city's roaring sway,
Lives the pulse of millions, one emergency away.
In the struggle, the strain, the silent plea,
Is the whispering hope, they will stay off the street.

A tragic accident, theft, disease or just losing work.
The cost of life increasing, antidepressants to fight hurt.
Mark these words now, no-one you know is immune.
From bankruptcy, homelessness and total ruin.
Most of us remain… One accident away.

-- Andrew Noske

No One Solution

Among the homeless population, no two people are the same. We hope the stories in this book demonstrate the diversity of this homeless pandemic. Some people have extreme health conditions, injuries, trauma, mental illness or addiction that put them onto the street. Some people want and are able to ask for help and others do not want or are unable to ask for help.

I personally believe there will never be one single solution that solves homelessness. Instead it will have to be a multitude of strategies and an effective way to determine what benefits each individual best.

Binary classifications are inherently flawed, but for the purpose of thinking about helping the homeless, we can imagine that most homeless people could be put onto a spectrum between recently displaced and chronically homeless.

1. Recently displaced

Most Americans live **paycheck to paycheck** with little if any reserve. So now imagine sustaining an injury or going into a coma to wake up evicted, all your possessions thrown away, and a five or six figure hospital bill that you can't pay. If this happened to you, would someone step up, pay your bills and keep all your personal and professional business afloat? Possibly not.

Recently displaced individuals often include people kicked out of home, fleeing domestic abuse, evicted families, recent release from jail or prison, mentally ill or even displaced by natural disasters like wildfires - which now ravage the wider bay area every year. In a **major natural disaster** or **war** an entire community is often destroyed. On a smaller scale a family car crash or something else disastrous can cause you to lose your entire support network in a flash.

Recently displayed people can be in a delusional state. Without any understanding of the streets they have a high chance of being robbed, raped, and beaten. Should they experience harsh treatment from law enforcement, they might categorize all police officers as adversaries, and thus, hesitate to seek their assistance. The world might seem against them, and yet, people who are the most recently homeless, are the ones most desperate and eager to get their lives back on track, to repay debt, to call on favors and ideally put a roof back over their head. The longer they stay on the streets, the more they move that needle towards never leaving.

2. Chronically homeless

We don't talk about this a lot, but some homeless people have no goals or dream of being in a house. How does that happen? It's similar to the process of being institutionalized in prison. Prisoners with long sentences (perhaps decades) usually get to the stage where they understand how to survive well in prison. There is a certain pride, they might build a network of friends, and the idea of being released back into a complex and changing outside world is actually terrifying. Would they even be accepted? Would anyone give them an honest job? Some might commit another crime deliberately just to return to prison.

For people who are homeless for long enough, they may start taking pride in learning how to survive the streets, in building a small network, or just surviving independently. Suddenly the idea of managing a bank account, taxes, electricity, health insurance, bills, finding and holding down a job in a competitive market, trying to afford rent in a competitive and expensive market. Overwhelming doesn't even cover it. Juggling all the things modern society requires, I have my own periods of feeling overwhelmed, and so the idea of starting from nothing - or from debt - down this complex dog-eat-dog adulting path gives me at least a small level of empathy.

Few people would consciously choose to sleep long term in a cold tent or cardboard box versus a roof with running water and toilets. However, when the world feels stacked against you, some people do feel that living in a car, sleeping bag or tent is just easier. Even those with fantastic well paid engineering jobs in San Francisco have started opting to do van-life versus paying exorbitant rent prices, and some of them will thus technically fall into the homeless category, but their numbers are still relatively few and people with good life savings are outside the scope of this book. Others still might do odd jobs and just opt for life in a car. A harsh life, but a simpler life.

Some of the Googlers I used to work with in the south bay had this idea that homeless people were just lazy. I don't think they understood that homeless people usually come from poverty, and even if they are able to find a job and work massively long hours, it probably won't be a well paid job, and they will still remain in poverty. It will just be poverty with a roof. Working ridiculous hours and sacrificing your health just for a roof doesn't feel much better than a tent. Why go through all that pain of a poorly paid job if you already have learnt to hustle the streets and not have to worry about a slumlord or potentially overbearing boss and a job that drains your soul. Why not just stay independent. It's not a lazy decision, it's almost a logical decision. Why fight the current?

You can take all these opinions for what they are worth, but the gradient between recently homeless and chronically homeless and homeless as a lifestyle is an important consideration. Don't assume every homeless person is able or wanting to get off the streets. If you want to know for sure then you'd have to talk to them. Understand how they got there, and what they might like to head towards. In my experience, many of the homeless people I've tried to approach outside of Haight Street are too deep into mental illness or depression to express dreams. When life beats you down so badly, hope might feel dangerous.

Your generosity to talk, to smile and offer just a little empathy or even fight local policy... that is where their hope might be rekindled. Someone to believe in them.

I met Ashel through a homeless man called Darrick. Darrick the drifter who often is seen on Haight street posing with one of his three amazing dogs on his back. Darrick has awesome tattoos and when I told him about my book he suggested I interview Ashel, and I'm glad I did. Ashel represents someone who has battled to get off the streets, but if well aware that they still live in poverty and they hope for a better life for all of their homeless friends.

The Story of:

Ashel: Adapting The Dragon

Born: 1988 (35 years old) in Orange, CA.

Pronouns: ze/then.

About: Ashley is a character-and-a-half - full of energy, humor and usually dressed as a friendly medieval dragon warrior. When I first met Ashley, they were wearing a badass Game of Thrones like outfit with a post-taxidermy coyote on their head. Ashey's dog, Rosie, was wearing awesome dragon wings, and was equally friendly to people. We'd just seen a self-driving car crash into the back of a bus just outside the famous "*Love on Haight*" street, so a few of us were sharing photos and we decided to do lunch.

Ashley's story is one of hope, but also what can go wrong in foster care. Ashley doesn't know their mum at all, and has no idea who their father is. They just know they were born near Los Angeles and at four years old were adopted into a conservative christian family in rural Oregon. Think 1800s conservative Christian out in the country. The only book they were allowed to read was the bible. Ashley's adopted mother had moderate mental issues and three biological children, already about to leave the nest, but then she suddenly adopted Ashley and then a younger brother to help do chores and live the good Christian life. This didn't bode well for either of the adopted kids. Ashely had an imagination, and their younger brother would later come out as gay. Food was "*bread, broth and bible*", and punishment was physical, but mostly psychological. At 11 years old, Ashley threw a toilet paper roller at their mother from the balcony, and for this misbehavior Ashley was promptly moved to a youth shelter where they remained for three days before they were thrown out for attempting witchcraft. Ashely laughs at the idea that they was the demon child for having imagination.

Sadly, Ashley's youth was being bounced between understaffed treatment centers where they were often shut into isolation, but ze still preferred it to home as they were allowed to read any books they wanted. At eighteen Ashley was put in a group home, but didn't stay long. Ashely decided to move to California, and remembers hitchhiking to the Haight area in a car with a hooker and her pimp, who said they needed to stop at a jail in Oakland along the drive. Ashley recalls that in 2012, Haight was a much different area. Full of character, deadheads and gangs. Each street corner had a cluster of people who stuck together and didn't necessarily welcome out-of-towners. These people were known as the "*Haighters*", but in spite of any gangs, there were still a lot of tourists who came. During those years Ashley enjoyed hitchhiking to new destinations and doing "*Rainbow Gatherings*" and medieval events.

Over the years since 2012, the homeless population fluctuated. At a couple of points, they would do a sweep to put all the homeless in Haight into community housing in the most sketchy area of the Tenderloin. Even if the intention was good, Ashley believes about half of them died because Haight has decent support against drugs among the homeless, but the Tenderloin is a known police-no-go-zone where hard drugs are rife and overdoses are a way of life. It effectively split the community.

Haight used to be a place where people would hang out in parks more, Ashley says in the last 10-15 years, lots of fences have been set up and Haight has almost no low income housing, except the rare place for a family. During the pandemic Ashley finally passed the infamous "*homeless test*"... A test who's algorithm is unknown, but which everyone readily agrees you have to lie to get in, and is more about "*who is houseable and might stay*" versus who might need it the most to survive. Somehow they were successful and in July 2022 was able to get into a shelter. Ashely has inspiration to leave however, because they still find it disheartening that their housing is more of a shelter where at least once a week they hear the sirens come to pick up another person from overdose. They also dream of getting their SSI back, because once you miss a check in it's hard to get back. Ashley's other big dream is to finish their transition from female to male, not really happy that people often refer to them as "*the woman with a big chest*".

What is the hardest lesson you learned on the streets: Don't make promises you can't keep. Homeless people often get promised help, but it usually doesn't come. For instance they'll be told "*housing*" when it's just a shelter, or a housing manager that never actually appears.

Something you are proud of: Being part of a big community of free thinkers. Including the rainbow gatherings community.

What tips might you offer someone newly homeless: Don't mess with another person's hustle. Whether they sell paintings, drugs, pan-handles, whatever, make sure you don't mess with their gig!

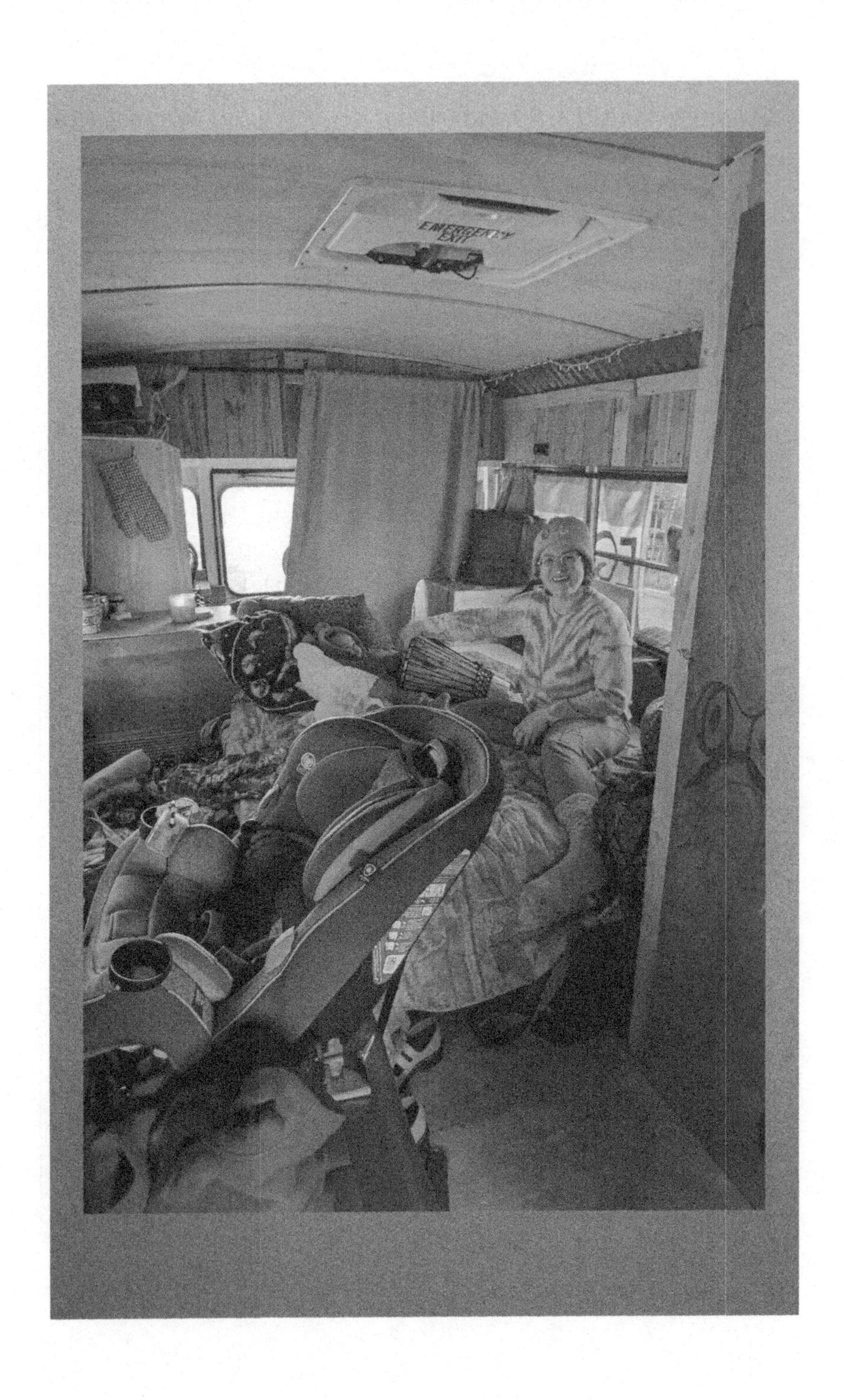
EMERGENCY
EXIT

Chapter 6: Another's Shoes

There is a beautiful and famous quote:

Do not judge a person until you've walked a mile in their shoes.

San Francisco often feels like a passive aggressive place to live, and while everyone acts very woke, all too many people judge the addict and homeless population as lazy or weak. As criminals. As inferior. We hope this book has already shed light onto the idea that if you were born into their shoes, you'd probably be in the same position, or worse. Many homeless people, in my experience, have an incredible resilience that I am not sure I would have in their circumstances.

While life is going well, it's very easy to frown down upon people who might turn to drugs and judge them. But for anyone who has been through a terrible life tragedy without support, or with the wrong people around, it's very easy to turn to a substance to numb the pain and find yourself on the street soon afterwards. The following two stories are not of addicts, but of two lovers who met and chose to live a simpler life in a van. To escape prejudice and oppression. To live positively and make the most of life, despite severe health conditions. This is the story of Timbre and her partner Murphy.

The Story of:

Timbre: Voice of the Angels

Born: 1996 (27 years old) in Lexington, South Carolina.

About: Timbre has the sweetest infection smile, sincere blue eyes and incredible resolve. What captures you about Timbre is a modest intelligence that some people might never expect someone homeless to be hiding, but I've spoken to enough homeless people to know better. With her background in writing, Timbre will impress you with the openness of her heart, her vulnerability and her eloquent wordplay. It wasn't a surprise to me when I heard that Timbre is a talented songwriter. Her first album on Spotify will make you sway with her angel-like chorus, and I highly recommend you to listen. I'm already excited for her next album. Timbre's backstory however, isn't entirely sweet.

Timber was born into a family of deep religion and homeschooling. Her mother and father were missionaries in the International Pentecostal Holiness Church, which meant a lot of travel and effectively begging each church for money. Timbre has a three year older sister who was taught piano, and Timbre would sing. Since pentecostal missionaries are not paid, the whole whole family would perform in song to help raise money for their next missionary adventure. Timber was born in South Carolina, but her childhood also took her living in South Africa, Australia and ten years of Singapore. This is the life that Timbre knew, but at eighteen years old she went to a women's college in South Carolina to become a creative and professional writer. Her parents returned to Singapore to recruit followers, and slowly fell out of touch. Homeschooled Timbre, meanwhile, excelled in school and was pretty much a straight A student. She told me she did well because she wanted to prove herself, but also realized that she didn't want to become a career professional, nor did she really get the chance. At 22 years old, Timber moved to Portland to help take care of her sister, who at this stage had showed mental illness and suicidal tendencies. Timbre recalls how terrifying it is to live with someone who you feared would have ended their own life each time you left the house and returned. It takes a huge emotional toll. Eventually her sister found a husband and started doing slightly better. Meanwhile Timbre started to fall in love with one of her friends, a charismatic black man called Murphy who she met at a concert. Unfortunately, Timbre's sister disapproved, and whether it was based on religion or race is inconsequential, Timbre was kicked out of the house and started traveling the road with Murphy.

Timbre laughed at the realization that she went so quickly to having *"a baby and a bus".* What she felt with Murphy was an unconditional love she never got from her family, and although she never expected to be living in a bus, she loves the fact that she can now travel on her own terms, and work on her art with the judgment from family. Timbre isn't totally sure if her parents know she is now a mother, and a couple of times in our interview got teary. That soon transferred to me being teary. Being homeless isn't easy, but I told her that between a loving life with little money, and a life with money but no love or fulfillment, she had chosen right with happiness.

What is the hardest lesson you learned on the streets: You are no different from your greatest fear. During her youth, Timbre was terrified of homeless people, her parents had always told her that they were dangerous, and that they were to lock the car doors when driving through certain neighborhoods. And now, of course, Timber is homeless. "*The most growth happens when you embody your deepest fear*".

Something you are proud of: (1) "*My little family*" and (2) "*My ability to adapt and change*".

What tips might you offer someone newly homeless: (1) "*Buy baby-wipes when you can, it's basically a shower in a bag*". (2) "*Try not to let people's disregards and disgust of you keep you from smiling at them anyway*". It is when Timbre said that last line I started to tear up. She basically was saying that some people out there will "*ask you not to exist*" once you become homeless. It's beyond being invisible, it's a form of prejudice just as toxic as racism. Yet somehow Timbre is and will remain a happy spark of light. Deeply thoughtful, and endlessly generous.

What are your aspirations: Timber has found a producer to work with, and is excited to work on her next album with a more professional setup versus her first album done in solo. She's never written a book before, but she'd love to write a children's book the explains epigenetics (obviously without the word epigenetics in the title) and together we came up with the idea for a children's book about homeless and compassion that we could call "*the dinosaur without a cave*". Her biggest dream, however, is to own land. Somewhere that she and Murphy can park the bus. In her nomadic childhood she never really felt like she had a home, and it was only at the end of the interview I noticed the tasteful tattoos on her knuckles read "*come home*".

To support Timbre Truth's Music:

- Link tree link: https://linktr.ee/timbretruth (Spotify etc)

The Story of:

Murphy: Staying in Love

Born: 1974 (49 years old) in Lompoc California.

About: Murphy, as a human, is just pure joy, laughter and fun. His laugh is infectious and he's one of the biggest characters you will ever meet. Being homeless doesn't have to cramp your style or your smile. His outfit is incredible, there are badges on all his clothes and a gold hat covering his awesome dreads. He also has some badass tattoos also and incredibly colorful custom shoes. In a strange way, I knew that someone this vibrant would have a colorful backstory with huge adversity. I was right.

Murphy was born in a small military backwater called Lompoc. A military brat, Murphy's step dad was in the air force, and they moved around. Murphy was eight when his step father committed suicide. They were supposed to move to Germany, but instead remained in a small military town. Murphy's biological dad was also in the military, but he only met his dad once at age 27 and never again.

Being in a small military town there is almost nothing to do, so in Murphy's words you either get into sports and school or you get into the streets. You pick "*square or streets*" and the streets were picked for him. At a very young age, Murphy was in the wrong place at the wrong time during a robbery and put in jail for the first time. He said this is when his strong distrust of the US government began. How could it not. At 16 years old she was tried as an adult for 707 - assault with a firearm. Luckily no-one was injured but he was sentenced 6 years and served 4. It was 1995 when he got out. Being institutionalized in prisons at such an early age really affects you. He said you quickly noticed the way police target certain communities. "*It wasn't even about racism*", he says, "*it was mostly classist*".

Murphy has two step sisters, one 4 years older and one 9 years younger and drug addiction was common where they grew up. Murphy says he's had several "*restarts of life*", but it was 3.5 years ago he met his primary partner, Timbre, at an open microphone night in Portland. After being friends for a year they fell in love and darted to drive around together. They largely stay in Portland, but often visit Haight, and also adore Ocean Beach in San Diego, stopping at Lompoc along the way to see family. Murphy loves that the Haight area is such a tight knit community. He can have moments where he might sleep on the sidewalk after a great night talking with new friends and making new connections, but usually he sleeps in his bus cuddled up with Timbre.

What is the hardest lesson you learned on the streets: You can't hold certain expectations... you learn to appreciate the space you do get and you learn to balance. He also loves the concept "*have less, share more*". The homeless community on Haight is especially good at sharing, when someone is in need the others rally and there is so much sharing. Over time he also realizes that he doesn't believe in stealing from big corporations or being negative towards anyone, because he just doesn't want that negative energy coming around him and his children.

Something you are proud of: Murphy is proud of his quality of life and becoming a more transparent person. He's also proud of his expensive shoes, but when you look closely you realize they are custom because Murphy has lost all his toes due to diabetes and health issues. He warns everyone he knows on the streets that if their toes ever change color you have to get it checked ASAP.

What tips might you offer someone newly homeless: "*Do the work on your mindset, and then you will be able to survive the streets*". "*Don't believe everything people tell you*". "*Keep your nose clean!*". Murphy joked that if 100 people he knew only stopped substances, especially alcohol, for a few months, they might be able to save enough for a small rural property to live together. That would be his hope for people. Sadly it's really hard for most people to see a path to "*get up*" out of homelessness. Murphy is an example of making it work. Being homeless and happy, with just enough coin to travel the country making friends.

What are your aspirations: Murphy's biggest dream is to create a successful sustainable traveling circus with other people in a similar place. 8 months travel, then 4 months rest, and building new equipment. He wants to always stay tapped in and aware of energy, to always be present with people and the community. Murphy also always aspires to become a better person and better parent.

Chapter 7: Spreading Happiness

This marks a turning point in our book. You can't look at homelessness without delving into drugs, death, loss and despair. But throughout are messages of hope. Occasionally people who are homeless make it off the streets, or in some cases remain homeless, but achieve a level of happiness that most rich people should be envious of.

If the meaning of life is truly happiness, then a lot of us should be asking how well we are going. In the United States, the emphasis has shifted from happiness towards success. Which means we are not truly happy until we feel we are winning in a competition to have more and more possessions and success. And this is causing people to be miserable.

Harmony is a girl who exudes happiness. I met her at an ecstatic dance event at the Church of Eight Wheels which is only 20 minutes walk east of Haight Ashbury. I had no idea she was homeless. We shared an amazing dance, we chatted and suddenly she mentioned that she was living in a van near Haight Ashbury. I was blown away and excited to interview her, and so later that week we went to coffee and talked about her life. This is Harmony's story.

The Story of:

Harmony: Messenger of Love

Born: 2002 (20 years old) in Dundil (near Niagara Falls) in Ontario Canada.

About: Harmony, also known as Rosemary, represents a fascinating demographic of homeless people. She lives in a bus. Homelessness for her is largely a lifestyle choice - she has the intelligence and youthful bounce that could probably land her a job back in Canada pretty easily, but she gets joy from traveling. I met Harmony out dancing, and soon learnt that Harmony is responsible for the many colorful chalk messages of love I see written for 100 meters down Haight street. Messages like "*you are loved*" and "*smile*". Harmony is like a beacon of sunshine, she dances, she blows bubbles.... and she just generally spreads love and smiles. Her spirit seems unbreakable, but her history is not all roses.

Harmony grew upon a small farm in Canada with her mother,

father and younger brother with many pets and exposure to nature. Her mum bred dogs. Her father, sadly, was a narcissist and drunk. Harmony learnt at a young age when her father switched from charming to abusive. She was only physically beaten badly a couple of times, but the verbal abuse was constant and her brother was beaten often. Maybe that explains why her brother is now into MMA and training to become a firefighter to help rescue people. Harmony's parents divorced when she was 14, and she said it was a huge relief to have him gone. Despite restraining orders, her father still manages to break into their property often and try to mess with her mother and her friends. Harmony and her brother try to have a good sense of humor about it. They both hope their mum can one day finally date again and find someone nice.

Harmony did well in school, getting into honors programs, and with all her friends interested in becoming air cadets she tagged along and was offered a full ride scholarship to become a pilot while still studying for high school. And that's when covid hit. Harmony wasn't able to graduate as normal - seeing her friends and staying goodbyes to her favorite peers and teachers. Instead she was studying at home and felt stir crazy. When restrictions were lifted she immediately traveled and had a revelation. She enjoyed the road.

People often work their whole lives so they have enough money to retire and drive around in an RV. Why not just start it now? Harmony bought an adorable blue bus that she calls Calypso. Her brother, who is also her best friend, and her mother worry about her, but she bought a wonderful dog called Zoso, who is a pit bull in case to help her stay safe when she's out and about on the street. She does note that San Francisco feels much less safe than other cities she's lived in, but she enjoys the hippie community here. When I asked her if she's a black sheep she told me she's a rainbow sheep. She also told me a story of almost losing Calypso after a rainstorm and together we set up a GoFundMe to help her repay some of the towing expenses.

What is the hardest lesson you learned on the streets: To "*do it your damn self*". The bus was her first time living alone, so she had to learn bus life, plus cooking, and learn to ask for help for car repair when needed.

Something you are proud of: Making people smile.

What tips might you offer someone newly homeless: Harmony says this next opinion comes from a place of "*relative privilege*". There are lots of programs cities have, and SF has many, but SF isn't great at helping in the right ways. What's tough is that as soon as people realize she doesn't have a home they can treat her as they do most homeless people. People in SF dissociate from the homeless - they don't see them as human, so don't expect anyone to help you if you are struggling for breath on the street. Learn to be self sufficient.

What are your aspirations: To buy a big piece of land in nature and start a community! To just "be", all the time... and to help others realize this life can be easy sometimes, not competitive and bleak. She wants others to know that instead of working years into retirement to travel, there's a good chance they can just travel now with an RV or with a car and a mattress in the back. Van life indeed!

Harmony was a wonderful breath of fresh air, and I felt important to include in this book because she represents someone enjoying the street life. There are moments she feels unsafe, but she builds her friends, she spreads her amazing chalk messages (messages I walk past all the time!) and goes to deadhead gigs with friends. I don't know what the future will hold for Harmony, but I'm excited to stay friends.

The most noticeable homeless people in San Francisco are those living in tents, or complex structures made of tarpaulin, cardboard, shopping carts, and other junk. What we are less likely to notice is a growing number of cars and vans parked on the street with bedding in the back. People often live in their car because it represents a portable option. I can't say this definitely, but among the youths who break into cars, they usually target tourists and seem to leave these "*live in*" cars and vans alone. I would like to imagine they do this as a code of ethics - not to rob people who are poorer than they are. Life in a car is brutal, uncomfortable and smelly, but offers better protection from the elements than a cardboard box.

The next person I interviewed has a small van setup with his boyfriend, and so is more comfortable than a car. Alex is a wonderful spark of hope, currently searching for work and I'm crossing my fingers for him. I saw Alex several times on the street before I finally timed it right to share a meal and an interview. It was an interview I really enjoyed. Alex to me represents youth and hope, not unlike Harmony and I was excited to introduce them and put them next to each other within this book. This is Alex's story.

The Story of:

Alex: Off the Straight Path

Born: Sep 2000 (23 years old)... birth town unknown, Illinois.

About: Alex grew up in several suburbs of Illinois where there wasn't much to do. Although he's unsure about the town he was born in, he remembers his childhood not being too bad initially. However, being an unplanned only child, his parents' deteriorating relationship made things increasingly difficult for him. With constant fighting and yelling, he struggled to do well in school. His mom worked in an elderly nursing home while his dad was a plumber. He even tried plumbing for a while with his dad, but the company started failing, and his dad lost his leg to an infection. Additionally, Alex realized that plumbing had some crazy laws that made it easy to be sued, so he decided that it wasn't for him to drone away as a plumber.

By age 20, Alex was living in Wisconsin and met a guy called Andrew online and they started dating. Alex describes Andrew in three words as easy-going, smart and goofy. They fell in love, and kept it pretty hidden at first. Alex said he realized he was in love when just after he saved Andrew's life. Andrew had some friends come over and they all did heroin, Alex had no idea that was happening, but was able to save Andrew from overdose and Andrew hasn't touched heroin since.

At home Alex had to watch as his mother became drunk. Her drinking got worse and worse, and Alex eventually realized it was not on him to watch her. He didn't want that poor life for himself. Andrew has an aunt in Haight-Ashbury and they also heard weed was cheaper in California, so they suddenly decided to try to escape.

When Alex and Andrew arrived in San Francisco, one and a half years ago, they had nothing. Worse, Alex lost his ID, which was a huge hassle trying to find work. During the time he didn't have an ID Alex said he was offered a couple of interesting jobs, but unable to take them. Eventually he got a van and now he has an ID he's hunting for work again. Alex said coming out of the closet wasn't too hard. He told his dad and his dad basically replied "*dude, I don't care, I just wanna see you*". Alex's dad decided to follow Alex's footsteps and try his luck in San Francisco also. Alex's father has told Alex's mum that Alex is gay, and apparently she seemed relatively cool with it, or perhaps she was just too inebriated to react.

Alex says he still feels really worried for his mum, but he knows there is not much he can do. Both sides of her family were drinkers, and he's not sure she has any chance of getting sober. Alex does really admire his dad though. He says life couldn't have been easy with a kid, a broken relationship and in an unsafe area of town, and it is surreal that his dad has followed Alex's footsteps and decided to live out of a car.

What is the hardest lesson you learned on the streets: "*Learning to take people's word less*". He said you have to understand that or you will be very let down on the street. Alex also noted that "*if you get a 'wrong' feeling in your gut, you should trust it*". He says that advice can save you.

Something you are proud of: "*Getting a van, since it's not easy* *to do something like that when you start with nothing*" and now "*starting to get more job interviews and call backs*". After waiting six months to get an ID, hopefully his moment will come.

What tips might you offer someone newly homeless: To make sure you never drink and get "*wet brain*", which is a very sad condition where the mind pretty much has gone. His other advice really surprised me. He said "*buy silver*". He says they keep their value and are just a useful asset to have and trade at a silver shop if you ever need to.

What are your aspirations: Alex says it's easy to get stressed about his life, but if he can find a paying job that is somewhat fulfilling, then things will fall into place. He also said he wants to do good for himself and others around him. Alex's aspirations are "*simplicity and security*". He wants to get to a point where he doesn't have to worry about his next meal.

Chapter 8: Solving Homelessness

When you read about the situation of the homeless in San Francisco it's easy to feel like it's hopeless. Despite pouring vast resources into combating homelessness little has improved in the last four decades of San Francisco's history. The combined city, state, and federal funding amounted to approximately one billion dollars for homelessness in the fiscal year of 2019-2020. Yet, the situation remains dire, raising questions about the effectiveness of current strategies. Where does the money go?

San Francisco residents became outraged when they realized that in these "*safe sleeping areas*" a single tent which might cost under a hundred dollars in material, costs the city on the order of $60,000 to build and maintain. Such figures were also published in "San Fransicko" by Michael Shellenberger[5], although it is not really obvious how many, if any, homeless people the author actually talked to in writing this book.

Housing First Fails

San Francisco's current model is a "*housing first*" approach that aims to provide immediate housing and then "*follow this up*" with support services. But those support services often never come. The costs and complications of housing often drain resources, neglecting the root causes. Without adequate support services, this model can fail those who need help most, including those grappling with mental health issues and addiction.

While "*housing first*" might seem an obvious solution, it ignores the multifaceted nature of homelessness. It doesn't address mental health issues or provide the necessary support services, causing many to return to the streets. It doesn't acknowledge that throwing a roof over someone's head technically makes them housed, but doesn't necessarily help save them from poverty. High costs and policy barriers exacerbate the housing crisis, making the construction of affordable housing challenging, and often discouraging the development of low-income housing.

A Support First System

As outlined in the amazing Beyond Homeless documentary.
A successful model to consider is San Antonio's "*Haven for Hope*." This initiative goes beyond a typical shelter, offering facilities for children, kennels for pets, and programs aimed at self-sufficiency. Since its inception in the mid 2000s, "Haven for Hope" has significantly homelessness (by as much as 80% in many areas) and served tens of thousands of people. Their success underscores the importance of a loving, compassionate approach in transforming lives. Unlike most homeless shelters, it is lively and full of color. It inspires hope. It is a place where each person serves and each staff member is recognized as different. They have collected every tool imaginable to ask people about their story and find out how to help. They have recognized that the key to to change a city is to change the culture. You need a culture of love and compassion.

"**Never doubt that a small group of thoughtful, committed citizens can change the world; indeed, it's the only thing that ever has**"
-- Margaret Mead

The "*Haven for Hope*" project started with a small collection of citizens, who noticed that - despite all the poverty they were seeing on the street - nobody seemed to be doing anything transformation in helping those homeless people thrive and reclaim independent lives. So people enrolled in that vision of a comprehensive solution that went to the root problem and promised to rescue tens of thousands of people. Their vision wasn't just "*we can reduce this statistic by giving people a bed*". Their vision was to listen to people and actually save them.

To truly address the homelessness crisis, San Francisco needs a mindset shift. Just patting someone on the back can light someone up. It can trigger transformation. What is really needed out there is compassion. For someone to believe in homeless people and invest in them properly, rather than the band aid solution of taking someone off the street for one night or one week only to see them back into the gutter. We need the residents of San Francisco to be humble enough to recognize that rich or poor, we are mirrors of each other. The person on the street is actually you. The person in the gutter is you with a poorer roll of the dice. That person is you.

At a city wide level, San Francisco needs policy change, for organizations to better collaborate in addressing the root cause of homelessness and not the symptom. At the level of an individual, what this city needs is compassion and hope.

Chapter 9: Fostering Hope

"Wherever you go, there you are"
-- Old Proverb

I wonder how many of us ask each other the beautiful question of service. "*How can I serve you?*"

You've already read about a solution that works at a city level, but it only works when people support and believe in each other. Believe in the greater goodness.

As this book comes to a close it's really obvious that our final interview can only be one person. Father Dan. Father Dan has never been homeless, but he is one of the most recognized and loved people in the neighborhood, by homeless and housed people alike. A warm and kind ally to every race, gender identity, sexual orientation and every minority group you could imagine. Regardless of your faith and position in life - poor or filthy rich - you will adore Father Dan. What's not to love about a beer loving priest who talks to everyone and spreads a message of love. There have been several articles written about Father Dan, but I specifically wanted to ask him about his life journey and his thoughts on the homeless population on Haight street. This is Father Dan's story.

The Story of:

Father Dan: Spreading Hope

Born: 1965 (57 years old) in Greenville, Michigan.

About: Father Dan is the most beautifully generous, liberal, and humble priest you could possibly imagine, and he feels gratitude for a terrific childhood. The youngest of six children, Dan grew up hunting and fishing on a beautiful eighty-acre farm in rural Michigan. It was a loving, church-going family where his father sold cars and his mother helped raise them all right on the farm. Dan took an early shine to his studies and felt the call to the priesthood as early as he remembered. However, he wasn't called to be celibate, so he left the seminary in his first year, got a degree in history, and went to work in clothing retail for fifteen years in Grand Rapids.

Father Dan didn't say this next part, but the story on the street is that he did very well in retail but sought out more meaning. At that point, he discovered the Episcopal Church and the call to ministry. He worked as a development director and fundraiser, then went to seminary, got ordained, and spent ten years in Benton Harbor, Michigan - a small city known for high poverty and crime - then six years in Flint - also known for high poverty and crime - and has now been in Haight for two years.

It really shocked me that Dan had only been in Haight-Ashbury for two years because so many people recognize him. Dan says he loves that every day is the same but different. He loves meeting the merchants, the homeless folk, housed residents, and even some of the tourists floating through. What makes Father Dan really incredible is that he intentionally spends much of his time walking his dog, Maggie, and hanging out on Haight Street, meeting people. He and his wife, Kate, are incredibly well known in the community. He says they felt really welcome and accepted early on.

Father Dan can often be found with a shot and a beer (his Michigan roots), hanging out in one of the local pubs or seeking live music wherever he can. When he first arrived in Haight, it was the tail end of the pandemic when you couldn't necessarily sit down to drink or eat, so he says it was a weird time to arrive. He is also aware that many people have been damaged by certain churches, so there is often a mistrust of authority. He makes sure he treads lightly and listens.

At that stage of the interview, Dan showed me that he has a pouch that always has dog treats and cigarettes as a simple but powerful way to break down barriers.

What brings you joy: "My wife, cooking a good meal, a beer, dancing... or seeing someone on the street you haven't seen for a while." It's relieving to see someone homeless who may have disappeared for a few months - just to know that they are still alive and doing okay. He said that paperwork is a drag, but that doesn't take much time. He loves all the other duties of ministry, and his congregation understands how important it is for him to be present on the street. He recalls the joy of seeing Smurf (Murphy) and Timbre leave then come back with a baby. He loves a good beer and conversation with Sonny and many others. Father Dan loves meeting people with or without homes who often possess remarkable educations and share deep theological conversations with him.

What brings you hope: "The incremental, sometimes painfully slow steps that I see when someone from one group intersects with someone from another group in a positive way." He refers to the tensions that can arise between merchants and housed people with the homeless people hanging out on the street corners. "People are afraid of what we don't know, and we keep ourselves distanced from what we are afraid of, and I see that so much in this neighborhood - perhaps going both ways - and if we can just stop and take the time to engage one-on-one and make eye contact - those types of interchanges give me hope." Father Dan is such a fan of people who extend friendliness and believes it is such a huge healing quality. If we can just figure out how to make eye contact, it would be incredible.

What is the hardest lesson you've learned: "Learning to slow down... and not try so hard to get my way." I begged Father Dan to teach me that lesson. He says he'd rather be happy than being right, but that wasn't always the case. As he's gotten older, he's gotten better at letting go.

Something you are proud of: Father Dan is proud of many things. In his personal life, he's proud of his four amazing children, who are all fiercely independent. Professionally, he's proud of discovering the benefits of "a ministry of presence". Just being visible has amazing dividends, which often means tempering huge ambition. Instead of always striving, he enjoys just being.

What tips might you offer someone newly homeless: "The most generous people tend to be the poorest." In the street mission in Grand Rapids, when someone came into the neighborhood, people helped refer others to resources. Ironically, the people who should feel scarcity the most can be the most generous and will help others learn how to survive and where to find what service. In Haight-Ashbury, some humility and generosity go a very long way. Father Dan likes to ask both the homeless and "upstairs people" (those with houses), "Why do you hang out here?" The answer is because of the history, because this was the nexus, there is still a vibe here, and this is where their friends hang out. "Folks lucky enough to have houses can invite them into their living room. If you are living in a tent or vehicle or SRO or sleeping in a doorway, where do you hang out? The intersection of Haight and Ashbury." Making friends with the regulars in this area bodes well to help combat loneliness and have more people to help lookout for you. That applies regardless of your housing status.

What is your vision and your aspiration in this community: "*It really goes back to breaking down those barriers.*" Unless you've been here pre-1967, one should get a bit of a sense of the history of the neighborhood and what it's like now. If you move into this neighborhood, you are moving into a place with hippie culture in its veins, and he wants to help people embrace that. In one way or another, "*everyone here is just trying to make it.*" Father Dan encourages everyone to take that little risk to look someone in the eye - maybe not at 2 in the morning, but at 2 in the afternoon - and you just might meet someone who brings a bit of joy into your life. If you always have earbuds on and your hat pulled down, you can effectively amplify loneliness in what is already a loneliness pandemic. It's so easy to be lonely in a densely populated area. What can bring us back to humanity is just a smile.

That is where the interview ended, and I was so excited that I recorded the whole interview on video because it let me be present instead of madly scribbling notes. Father Dan then took me on a great tour of the church - the "All Saints' Episcopal Church" on 1350 Waller St, which I also filmed. After that, we did the short walk to grab a muffuletta at Sandy's on Haight Street and then a couple of beers at the Gold Cane. You couldn't help but notice Father Dan knew everyone by name. He might ask about their kids or something else going on in their life. It's refreshing to see someone treat everyone the same. We stopped to give a cigarette to Oreo - a young homeless kid on a skateboard who I remembered from interviewing Tony B, who came up with a smile to get a couple of cigarettes. Father Dan chatted to a guy lying on the sidewalk with the same kindness and reverence as he did to a lovely woman and her kids who were passing the church. He also knew everyone in the bar, and we all made jokes about life. I apologized to Father Dan for saying "Jesus" a couple of times, but he said he really wasn't bothered and was known to drop the occasional profanity himself. Father Dan is wonderful in his genuine kindness to everyone and his relatability. He introduces people to each other, tells stories, but most importantly, he listens. He cares. I couldn't think of anyone else more fitting to end the book, and I'm excited to hit publish and show him the finished product.

Many books about homeless people, and many homeless organizations have a religious agenda. I want it to be clear this book has none. No matter what you believe in, the very best humans are those who don't turn a blind eye to members of their own community who are dying on the street.

Of all the wonderful things you can do for a homeless person. The value of just acknowledging their humanity is immeasurable. As Sonny would say... the power of a good deed is "overwhelming". In times when you feel sorry for yourself and your struggles, remember that others have it worse, and need love even more than you. Perhaps helping others is the pathway to happiness you seek.

My hope with this book is hard to summarize into one sentence, but we will try to summarize it in a paragraph. We want people to care. We want other people to be inspired to write similar books about other cities. I want the people who I interviewed to prosper. WeI can't guarantee this book will become popular, but we want to print hundreds of copies so that people on the street can give away or sell copies for a small amount of money to buy food. But really the important thing is that people read the book and resonate with this message of giving a damn. Of caring. You already have the tools to affect change. You just have to use them. We will finish this book with words we have used already.

We want the residents of San Francisco to be humble enough to recognize that rich or poor, we are mirrors of each other. The person on the street is actually you. The person in the gutter is you with a poorer roll of the dice. That person is you.

Please be human and help all people feel seen and loved. Be kind, and help us break down the barriers to help people who have been knocked down get back up onto their feet. It starts with a smile.

A Thank You From the Authors

This book was a labor of love. It's not intended for any profit to the author, in fact it will lose money. We created a GoFundMe for James to get a scooter, but with the leftover money we will buy many copies of this book to give to homeless people to distribute to whoever will take it and read it.

This book isn't meant to be polished. It is raw. That said, if you want to help us make it better, or write a version for your own neighborhood please reach out!

We have a huge thank you to the people who we interviewed, to those who supported us, to the Atlas Project (which Andrew was part of), but most of all to you.

We thank you for reading this book.

For opening your heart. Our humble request is that if you got this book for free, or even if you bought a copy for a few dollars, that you go onto Amazon and leave an honest review and order a copy for a friend who you might benefit from.

Sincerely,
Andrew and James

PS: Learn more about this book, order more copies or read more without-a-home stories via: ***www.withoutahome.net***

About the Authors

Andrew Noske, PhD

Andrew Noske got his PhD in diabetes research at the Institute for Molecular Bioscience in Australia, before moving to the United States to pursue a postdoc in neuroscience then a left turn into software engineering at Google Maps. He currently lives in San Francisco, and his biggest passions are dancing, the environment, writing, human psychology and trying to make an impact in the United States.

James Richardson

James Richardson is a glassblower and his story is the first one in the book. Since writing started, James has been able to get off the streets and move in with a friend. He delivers for Uber Eats on his scooter and now that he has acquired a set of glass blowing equipment he is hoping to make glass blowing his main hustle and see his daughter again soon.

References

Books:

1. Babcock, T. M. (2017). *Helping the Homeless: A Service Guide.*
2. The U.S. Department of Housing and Urban Development (2022). *The 2022 Annual Homelessness Assessment Report (AHAR) to Congress.*
3. ASR (2022). *San Francisco Homeless Count and Survey, 2022 Comprehensive Report.*
4. O'Connell, J. J. (2005). *Premature Mortality in Homeless Populations: A Review of the Literature.*
5. Shellenberger, M. (2021). *San Fransicko: why progressives ruin cities.* First edition. New York, NY, Harper, an imprint of HarperCollins Publishers.

Websites & Movies:

6. Andrew Noske (2018). *Strawberries for Smiles.* www.strawberriesforsmiles.com
7. Beyond Homeless. (2022). *Beyond Homeless: Finding Hope.* In Beyond Homeless. Retrieved from www.beyondhomeless.org
8. Invisible People. (2023). *Invisible People Videos.* Retrieved from https://invisiblepeople.tv
9. Andrew Noske. (2023). *Without a Home Project.* Retrieved from www.withoutahome.net

Made in the USA
Las Vegas, NV
15 June 2023

73471784R00056